SUPER
EMILIE COLLYER

CURRENCY PRESS
The performing arts publisher

CURRENT THEATRE SERIES

First published in 2025
by Currency Press Pty Ltd,
Gadigal Land, Suite 310, 46–56 Kippax Street, Surry Hills, NSW 2010, Australia
enquiries@currency.com.au
www.currency.com.au

in association with Red Stitch

Copyright: *Super* © Emilie Collyer, 2025.

COPYING FOR EDUCATIONAL PURPOSES

The Australian *Copyright Act 1968* [Act] allows a maximum of one chapter or 10% of this book, whichever is the greater, to be copied by any educational institution for its educational purposes provided that that educational institution [or the body that administers it] has given a remuneration notice to Copyright Agency [CA] under the Act.

For details of the CA licence for educational institutions contact CA, 12 / 66 Goulburn Street, Sydney, NSW, 2000; tel: within Australia 1800 066 844 toll free; outside Australia 61 2 9394 7600; fax: 61 2 9394 7601; email: memberservices@copyright.com.au

COPYING FOR OTHER PURPOSES

Except as permitted under the Act, for example a fair dealing for the purposes of study, research, criticism or review, no part of this book may be reproduced, stored in a retrieval system, or transmitted in any form or by any means without prior written permission. All enquiries should be made to the publisher at the address above.

No part of this book may be used or reproduced in any manner for the purpose of training artificial intelligence technologies or systems without the express written permission of the author and the publisher.

Any performance or public reading of *Super* is forbidden unless a licence has been received from the author or the author's agent. The purchase of this book in no way gives the purchaser the right to perform the play in public, whether by means of a staged production or a reading. All applications for public performance should be addressed to the author c /— Currency Press.

Typeset by Brighton Gray for Currency Press.
Cover image shows Caroline Lee, Lucy Ansell and Laila Thaker.
Cover design by Mathias Johansson for Currency Press.

Currency Press acknowledges the Traditional Owners of the Country on which we live and work. We pay our respects to all Aboriginal and Torres Strait Islander Elders, past and present.

A catalogue record for this book is available from the National Library of Australia

Contents

S<small>UPER</small> 1

Theatre Program at the end of the playtext

This work was written and first produced on the unceded lands of the Wurundjeri peoples of the Kulin Nation.

Super was first performed at Red Stitch Actors' Theatre, Euro-Yroke, Boon Wurrung Country, St Kilda, Melbourne, on 11 June 2025, with the following cast and creatives:

PHOENIX	Lucy Ansell
RAE	Caroline Lee
NEL	Laila Thaker

Director/Dramaturg, Emma Valente
Set & Costume Design, Romanie Harper
Lighting Design, Natalia Velasco Moreno
Sound Design, Beau Esposito
Associate Director, Cassandra Fumi
Assistant Set & Costume Design, Dylan Lumsden
Stage Manager, Ellen Perriment
Assistant Stage Manager, Kara Floyd

CHARACTERS

RAE
PHOENIX
NEL

Who all have superpowers. These are very real and have genuine superpower impact in this world, so should be played as such.

These characters are written with feminised bodies in mind but can be played by anyone. Please feel free to adjust pronouns if required.

I encourage anyone producing and casting this work to consider performers from a wide range of backgrounds, including people with diverse ethnic and cultural backgrounds, different ages, and people with disabilities.

SETTING

A community room / hall / space where they hold support meetings.

TIME

The play is set around about now. Events take place some time between a few months and a year. Time gets strange.

This playtext went to press before the end of rehearsals and may differ from the play as performed.

ONE

NEL *and* PHOENIX *are setting up for a meeting. Maybe sweeping, getting cups ready, general prep activities.* PHOENIX *might be doing little bits of stretching.* NEL *is finishing off eating something fast-food-y.*

PHOENIX: Swimming. Running.
NEL: It is a holiday. For relaxation and fun.
PHOENIX: Running is fun! 5K tops.
NEL: Hm. Remember last time?
PHOENIX: You did very well.
NEL: I walked half of it.
PHOENIX: But you tried! I was so proud. And you said you wanted to get fit.
NEL: I said I *should* get fit. I've scheduled bird watching. Moon birds!
PHOENIX: Eastern Curlews are wild migratory birds, Nel. I can't promise they'll appear.
NEL: Well, they're scheduled.
PHOENIX: [*laughing*] Great. Oh! Surfing too. Around four is the best time.
NEL: Then afternoon tea?
PHOENIX: A.m.
NEL: You are joking.
PHOENIX: I am not. Best time of day. I can't wait! Open road. The great outdoors. Car. Tent. Done.
NEL: About that ...

She has her phone out.

PHOENIX: What?
NEL: I found a gorgeous gastro pub that also has a special on accommodation. Sea views. Real beds!
PHOENIX: There are sea views from the tent.
NEL: Hm. Oh—it's ten. Let's put a pin in this.

Beat.

Super!

The word SUPER is how they start the support part of their weekly meeting and how they remind themselves of their core purpose.

PHOENIX: Super!
NEL: We hold our powers with care.
PHOENIX: We strive to do no harm.
NEL: We hope to make the world a better place.
TOGETHER: We take small steps with big hearts.

    RAE *enters*.

RAE: Hello?
PHOENIX: It's in the small meeting room, One-B, around the back.
RAE: What is?
PHOENIX: AA.
RAE: I'm not looking for AA.
PHOENIX: Sorry then, we can't help. If you don't mind?
NEL: Oh my god.
RAE: I saw this pamphlet: 'Have you experienced bodily occurrences that have an impact on others?'
NEL: Oh. My. God.
RAE: I am in the right place?
NEL: Yes. Absolutely. That is our pamphlet. The superpower support group. This is our group.
PHOENIX: You're looking for the superpower support group?
RAE: I am.
NEL: Welcome! Welcome!
PHOENIX: The meeting did start at ten.
RAE: I was here at ten.
PHOENIX: Well, not quite, because we'd already started.
NEL: It can be hard to find.
PHOENIX: Giant sign that says 'Community Room'.
NEL: Anyway, you're here now. Which is amazing!
PHOENIX: And you are?
RAE: I'm Rae.
PHOENIX: Hello. I'm Phoenix.
NEL: And I'm, oh my god, who am I? I can't even.
PHOENIX: This is Nel.
NEL: I love you. I mean, I literally own every one of your books and I never miss your show and you are, you are. You are amazing.
RAE: Thank you, that is so kind.

PHOENIX: We just have a form here for you to fill out.
RAE: Oh, I'd rather not.
NEL: No, we don't.
PHOENIX: It's your form, Nel, you made the form.
NEL: I know but Rae doesn't have to fill in forms. She's ... Rae.
RAE: Just confidentiality. In my line of work.
NEL: Of course, of course.
PHOENIX: Your line of work?
NEL: Oh my god, Phoenix, do you literally live under a rock?? *Rae's Sunshine Cooking. Meals for a Rainy Day. Be Your Own Rae in the Kitchen.* I'm a card-carrying Beamer! I know you must get this all the time, but would you mind if I got a photograph?
RAE: I'd rather not.
NEL: Of course. Silly me. Yes. This is a safe space.
PHOENIX: I don't watch television.
RAE: Good for you.
NEL: I do! I love it. I love you.
PHOENIX: She knows.
RAE: So this is it?
NEL: We are small but mighty!
RAE: I've rather over-catered.
NEL: Catered?

RAE has treats, something expensive/elegant looking.

RAE: Just a small gesture, something to contribute.
NEL: Oh. My. God. Are these? They are. Lemon Zest Snaps. [*Eating one*] Oh my god. This is heaven in my mouth. Phoenix, you have to try one.
PHOENIX: I'm okay, thanks.
NEL: That's fifty dollars' worth of biscuit there, and worth every cent, Rae! Can I get you a coffee?
RAE: I'd love a short black, thank you.
NEL: Oh god. We only have instant. I can pop out.
RAE: [*referring to* NEL*'s fast food*] I didn't see any cafés nearby. Only ...
NEL: Oh god, that's embarrassing.
RAE: Not at all.
NEL: I just—I get very hungry.

RAE: Of course. They're very convenient. But please, Nel, don't go to any trouble.
NEL: I can't believe you know my name. Nobody ever remembers my name.
PHOENIX: What am I?
NEL: Sorry. I mean anyone important.
PHOENIX: Not getting better.
NEL: Famous! That's all. You know I love you. But this, well, Rae. Rae. Look at me, casually saying your name. Ha! Rae, we've been waiting for a long time for others to join us.
PHOENIX: Yeah. A long time. So, Rae ... why are you here?
RAE: Well, Phoenix, when I saw that pamphlet, it seemed like it was really speaking to me. [*Quoting the pamphlet*] 'Do these bodily phenomena make you feel strange but also powerful?' And they do! My doctor said hormones and my PA thought allergies. But I've always been very attuned. I follow my instincts, my bliss.
PHOENIX: Of course you do. We have a few questions, protocols.
NEL: Just one. Tell us about your—
PHOENIX: [*cutting her off*] Bodily phenomenon.
NEL: Phoenix.
PHOENIX: We don't know yet.
NEL: Rae. Tell us—what happened?
RAE: So as you know, I work in television.
PHOENIX: I don't watch television.
NEL/RAE: We know.
RAE: I had a meeting. A visioning session.
PHOENIX: What's a visioning session?
RAE: I had a new concept. Chutney. Preserves.
NEL: Oh my god. Brilliant.
PHOENIX: I'm never sure about chutney. Sweet? Savoury? It's confused.
NEL: I love it.
PHOENIX: Of course you do.
NEL: Keep going, Rae. So you're in this meeting ...
PHOENIX: Seeing visions.
RAE: Visioning.
NEL: Dreaming up new ideas right?

RAE: Exactly. And let me tell you, my ideas have made that network a *lot* of money.
NEL: You're their star!
RAE: And they say to me, those numbskull TV execs, they say chutney's not testing with their demographic. They say: 'It's for old people.' They say: 'We're going in another direction.'
NEL: What?
PHOENIX: So?
RAE: And I ... Oh. Oh. Here it comes.

> RAE *starts to cry.* PHOENIX *and* NEL *start crying as well, automatically, strangely.*

NEL: [*crying*] I can't believe they did that to you.
RAE: [*crying*] Don't they know who I am?
PHOENIX: [*crying*] I don't care!
RAE: [*crying*] And this happened. In the meeting.
PHOENIX: [*crying*] What?
NEL: [*crying*] The crying?
RAE: [*crying*] The crying! I couldn't stop.
PHOENIX: [*crying*] I can't stop.
RAE: [*crying*] And they all, they all started crying too!
NEL: [*crying*] Of course they did!
PHOENIX: [*crying*] Why can't I stop?
RAE: [*crying*] My replacement was twenty years old!
PHOENIX: [*crying*] Why do I suddenly want a biscuit?
NEL: [*crying*] They're idiots to replace you, Rae! I'll start a petition!
PHOENIX: [*crying*] What the ... No ... I ...

> PHOENIX *struggles to release herself from the crying 'spell'. She summons up her own power and sucks the emotions right out of* NEL *and* RAE, *who stop crying immediately and collapse into a soft, neutral heap, as if tranquilised.*

RAE: What ... is ... happening?
NEL: Phoenix! Stop it!

> NEL *struggles to release herself from* PHOENIX*'s power, but rallies.*

Everybody, just—okay.

NEL *enacts her powers. As* NEL *utters the following words, the others snap out of their torpor and into action. The items magically appear, perhaps in their hands.*

Tissues. Tea. Incident report form. Are you okay? Rae?
RAE: Yes I feel … efficient.
NEL: Phoenix?
PHOENIX: I'm okay.
NEL: I don't really care that you're okay. I care that you exerted your superpower on Rae, and me, without warning or consent.
PHOENIX: So did she!
NEL: Yes, but she was unaware. It's all new to her. You know we can't use the powers on each other.
PHOENIX: You did it too.
NEL: I was rescuing the situation.
PHOENIX: [*mimicking* NEL] You were rescuing the situation.
NEL: Would anybody like to file a formal complaint?
RAE: No, I …
PHOENIX: No.
NEL: Excellent. Paperwork filed. Everybody is calm.
RAE: Did you say I have a superpower?
NEL: Yes.
PHOENIX: Well, she cried.
NEL: You felt it, Phoenix.
RAE: My doctor said estrogen. Too much? Not enough. Something.
NEL: It's a superpower.
PHOENIX: Maybe.
RAE: So the powers aren't like the ones in the movies? Super-strength and flying and X-ray vision?
PHOENIX: The movies are bullshit. Boys with toys. Fucking Marvel.
NEL: Our powers, Rae, are about making things better, helping people. Mine are administrative. I make ordinary, necessary things happen so efficiently it can feel like time speeds up. Tea. Tissues. A seat.
RAE: Yes. That was amazing. And yours, Phoenix?
NEL: Phoenix sucks powerful emotion out of situations. It's usually anger but as we just saw, it can be anything.
RAE: That's why I felt numb.
PHOENIX: Calm. It's calming.

RAE: It was numb. I didn't much like how it felt.
PHOENIX: Things don't have to feel good to be good for you.
RAE: And where do you use your administration and ... calming powers? Just here?
PHOENIX: Oh my god.
NEL: We keep very busy. For example, we are in the heart of football season now, so I zip around to all the community clubs making sure they're running efficiently. Uniforms. Rosters. Oranges. Kids' sport is so important! I love helping out.
PHOENIX: I go to the big games to suck out anger from losing fans so they don't get home and kick the shit out of their families.
NEL: You okay, P?

PHOENIX *is a bit wobbly; the work does affect her emotionally.*

RAE: That does sound busy.
NEL: Every weeknight and weekend! It's a *lot* fitting it in around work.
RAE: So it's like a hobby.
PHOENIX: It's not a hobby. It's a calling. A power. And we have plans. The amount of good we'll be able to do if we can get into places like government. Corporations.
RAE: And ... my power?
NEL: Amazing.
PHOENIX: But what does it actually do?
NEL: It made you want a biscuit. It made me want to start a petition. Which I still do, by the way!
RAE: Oh, they didn't sack me.
PHOENIX: They what?
RAE: After the crying, they changed their minds. Fully committed to the chutney show—*Preserve This!*
NEL: Wow. It changed them. Also—great name!
PHOENIX: I don't know.
NEL: It's a clever play on words.
PHOENIX: Not the show, the whole thing.
NEL: We don't own the powers, Phoenix.
PHOENIX: I know.
NEL: We see the potential. We nurture the power. I saw you ... defuse road rage in the car park. Thelma noticed my spreadsheet skills. And Thelma's guide with her, and so on.

RAE: Thelma? Should I meet Thelma? Is she in charge?
PHOENIX: Ha.
NEL: Thelma died.
RAE: Oh, I'm sorry.
NEL: It's not your fault! We've all been guided. If we don't notice the powers they don't develop. If we don't use them, they are forgotten.
PHOENIX: It's just us. And nobody is 'in charge'.
RAE: You seem to be assessing whether I'm worthy or not.
PHOENIX: I don't think someone like you should have a superpower.
RAE: Someone like me? A chef?
PHOENIX: A celebrity.
RAE: Aha.
PHOENIX: Power on top of all that power is unfair. Our work is to help humanity and we don't need a celebrity for that.

    RAE *looks around as if this all could do with a bit of shine.*

RAE: Well ...
PHOENIX: We're grassroots.
RAE: You just said you want to expand.
NEL: We do!
RAE: I can definitely help with that. I'm very good with growth.
NEL: Phoenix?
RAE: Am I in?
PHOENIX: Can you follow guidelines?
RAE: Of course!
NEL: Of course! This is amazing! Welcome! Ooh, we're going away! A staff retreat. You should come!
RAE: I can cook.
NEL: Oh my god. How exciting is this?! Rae! *The* Rae. A superhero!!
PHOENIX: We don't use that word. It can lead to hubris, which can lead to errors.
NEL: Okay, yes. Rae, we are not superheroes.
RAE: Noted.
NEL: But we kind of are. Just a little bit.
RAE: Just a little bit of a motherfucking goddamn superhero.

TWO

NEL, PHOENIX *and* RAE *are dressed pretty flash. They are the judges on a new reality TV show,* So You Think You Have a Superpower?*, and they are having their weekly meeting just before the first night of live filming.*

NEL: [*admiring their outfits*] Wow!
RAE: Right?
PHOENIX: We're very ... bright.
RAE: We look fantastic! The network *love* us and the concept. They're expecting at least one million viewers.
NEL: What if I freeze? What if I do that thing? I kept doing it during rehearsal. I can't help it, the camera is just there, and I lock onto it.
RAE: It's called barrelling, and don't worry about it.
NEL: So many cameras. The cables are all secure, yes? Good O, H and S?
RAE: Very secure. Just focus on us and the contestants.
NEL: And the live audience. And the one million viewers.
RAE: You won't be able to see them.
PHOENIX: Can we please stop saying one million?
RAE: It's fine. It's going to be great.
NEL: Okay. Time to start. Super!
PHOENIX/RAE: Super!
VOICE FROM OFF: Ladies, you're on in ten.
RAE: Thanks, Steve!
NEL: Alright, let's keep it moving.
PHOENIX: We're not rushing it though. We do not rush check-ins.
RAE: I'm still not sure why we scheduled a check-in right before our first live show.
PHOENIX: I'm still not sure about filming the live show in our community space.
RAE: The network's crazy for the grassroots vibe.
NEL: I love it! Sharing our space with the world.
PHOENIX: They've turned the main hall into a TV studio.
RAE: Minor changes.
PHOENIX: Tell that to the Spin for Seniors class. They kicked them out.

NEL: Oh, they're fine! They've been relocated to the futsal courts. They can learn some new skills! Now. Clock's ticking. We all agree weekly meetings are vital. It's tight but we can do it.
RAE: Alright. Super!
PHOENIX: Don't say it like that. Aggressively.
NEL: It's okay, Phoenix, it's just a word.
PHOENIX: But we have to do it right.
NEL: Let's all take a moment. Breathe. Do you want to sit?
PHOENIX: I can't.
NEL: You're wound up, I see that.
PHOENIX: No, I literally can't. They sewed me into this thing. I can barely move.
RAE: You look amazing.
PHOENIX: Very funny.
RAE: I'm not joking. You're stunning.
NEL: That's lovely, Rae. Phoenix, Rae just paid you a lovely compliment.
PHOENIX: Thank you, Rae.
NEL: Now. Let's start.
PHOENIX: Okay. Super!
NEL/RAE: Super!
PHOENIX: We hold our powers with care.
NEL: We strive to do no harm.
RAE: We have big heads and small hearts.
PHOENIX: Nel!
RAE: Sorry.
NEL: It's okay. We're all a bit stressed. We take small steps, with normal-sized heads and big hearts. Yes?
ALL: We hope to make the world a better place.
RAE: Fab. Let's go.
PHOENIX: Challenges.
RAE: Oh my god.
PHOENIX: We do this every week.
RAE: I know. I thought this week we might move it along since we are literally about to launch a new television show.
PHOENIX: We do it properly—or I'm not going on.
RAE: Really?
PHOENIX: Really.

NEL: As I have said, *so* many times now, we have time. Or we do, if you two stop bitching. Challenges. Rae.
RAE: Phoenix.
NEL: No, you first.
RAE: She's my challenge.
PHOENIX: Nice.
NEL: This is a safe place for honest sharing. Rae, can you talk about this with constructive, non-accusatory 'I-based' statements? In less than two minutes.
RAE: I sometimes find Phoenix's negative attitude confronting.
PHOENIX: I'm not negative. I have standards.
NEL: Phoenix, I know this is hard but let Rae speak her truth and then you can speak yours.
PHOENIX: Will I get two minutes?
NEL: We will all get the same. It's scheduled. Rae.
RAE: We *all* agreed to do the show, after a lot of very hard work on my part negotiating with the network.
PHOENIX: We voted. I respect rules.
RAE: But she was still so endlessly reluctant, pointing out every flaw.
PHOENIX: Somebody has to make sure the powers are not disrespected.
NEL: Phoenix, *please*.
RAE: And when I saw her final BTS content I was like, Oh my god.
NEL: What did she say? What did you say?
PHOENIX: In my 'Between the Stars' interview—
NEL: Between the stars?
RAE: Behind the scenes. BTS. But I'm glad you're seeing yourself as a star.
PHOENIX: I'm not! I don't know the lingo like you do. I don't watch television.
RAE/NEL: We know.
PHOENIX: Anyway, I said I think the whole thing is a ridiculous idea, that we'll never find people with true superpowers this way. It's not a competition, it's a calling.
NEL: You said that?
RAE: It's brilliant!
NEL/PHOENIX: What?
RAE: Every talent show needs the arsehole judge.

PHOENIX: I'm not an arsehole.
RAE: The purist. Competitors will be dying to impress you. Audiences will adore you.
PHOENIX: Have you seen the 'superpowers' people have listed?
NEL: Of course I have.
PHOENIX: Knowing when to cut an avocado open. Knowing how much food any social situation requires. Noticing someone has changed their hair. Always mixing the right amount of cordial. Choosing gifts for teenagers.
RAE: That *is* hard.
NEL: I know, right? I mean, they just want cash but that's so boring. And if you *do* get it right you feel like a goddamn rock star.
RAE: This woman apparently has a service—all of her friends use it. Never fails.
NEL: [*to* PHOENIX] See! There are so many interesting things. Remembering birthdays. Finding lost car keys. Unjamming photocopiers. Keeping indoor plants alive.
PHOENIX: I'm not saying these aren't handy skills. But superpowers?
NEL: They might be! Remember, Phoenix, we had to have someone notice ours and nurture them. Small things can become very powerful.
RAE: Keeping indoor plants alive, yes. Putting spiders outside, amazing. Folding fitted sheets.
NEL: Incredible! I just scrunch mine up and throw them in the cupboard. This one is lovely: cool hands when hot, warm hands when cold.
RAE: I tend to be the one who sees the snake. Hm.
NEL: Maybe she can help us learn how to live with animals more ethically?
RAE: It's great! We need some weird and wacky ones, a couple of duds.
PHOENIX: Isn't that just mean? These people really hope coming on a show like this is going to, like, transform their life.
RAE: That's how these shows work. People know what they've signed up for.
PHOENIX: Despite what you think, I actually don't want to humiliate anyone. I want to do things ethically.
NEL: You were happy to humiliate me.

    Beat.

PHOENIX: What?
NEL: The show is 'a ridiculous idea'.
PHOENIX: Nel, you've always known I had doubts about the show.
NEL: Yes, but that's different from telling the whole world how stupid you think I am.
PHOENIX: Not you, Nel! I don't think you're stupid.
NEL: I *love* the show. I can't wait to meet the amazing people who put themselves forward with their beautiful skills, who want to make the world a better place.

Beat.

So. My challenge is being hurt by my best friend. I'm dealing with it by reminding myself that we are all flawed but all deserve to be super. Done in ten seconds. See, ladies—that's what efficiency looks like. Phoenix. Your turn. What challenges have you faced this week?
PHOENIX: Well, I …
NEL: Aside from hating the stupid show.
RAE: Nel, shall we let Phoenix speak her truth?
PHOENIX: I am … [*Perhaps placatory*] finding these eyelashes a bit tricky.
RAE: Don't touch them. Once the glue fully sets you won't feel your eyelids anymore and that helps.
NEL: Thank you, Rae, for helping Phoenix meet her challenge. Phoenix, do you feel your challenge has been met?
PHOENIX: Yes.
RAE: If I may …
NEL: You have had your turn, Rae, and time really is pressing.
RAE: I want to move us to gratitude.
NEL: Oh. Yes. Good.
RAE: I feel grateful to you both. Nel, for your enthusiasm. Phoenix, for your honesty. The beauty of television is that it takes small things—like your support group, which we agreed was a little closed-off and elitist—and creates possibility. Nel?
NEL: I'm grateful for Imodium. I really don't want to do a nervous poo live on air. Phoenix?
PHOENIX: I'm grateful … for my friend. Who wants to make the world a better place.

VOICE FROM OFF: Talent walking in one minute, please!
NEL: Eek! I've been practising. Is it: 'So you *think* you have a superpower?' OR 'So *you* think you have a superpower?'
RAE: Both are great.
NEL: Oh my god, I'm going to sweat all over these amazing clothes.
RAE: That's okay, you'll have a new outfit each show.
PHOENIX: That's a waste.
NEL: They're ethically made. Yours is vegan. We made sure of that.
RAE: Brands will be dying to dress you. The show has so much buzz. My old network was desperate to get in on it. Shame they were 'going in that other direction'.
PHOENIX: So this is just about payback for you?
RAE: No. But it doesn't hurt.
PHOENIX: And you're sure … I don't look stupid?
NEL: Oh my god, stop it! You look incredible.
RAE: You really do. I've got a sneaky feeling.

The sound of an audience being warmed up and a VO announcement:

VO: Are you ready to find out? The question we've all been dying to ask: *So You Think You Have a Superpower?* It's time to meet our *super*star judges for the very first time, we're live from the place where all the magic happens, say hello to your new favourite miracle makers: *Nel*, *Rae* and *Phoenix*!

THREE

RAE, NEL *and* PHOENIX *are probably wearing very big robes or something similar.*

There may be soft music or whale sounds.

After a while, RAE *screams.*

Then NEL *also screams.*

Then PHOENIX *screams.*

A luxurious pause.

RAE: Excellent scream work, everyone.

Some more pleasurable silence.

You should have come to Iceland, Phoenix. They have amazing birds there.
PHOENIX: It clashed with training.
NEL: How was Ethiopia?
PHOENIX: Incredible. Those runners are elite.
NEL: How are your lumps?
PHOENIX: Growing faster and more of them. Training helps. I can literally see them deflate when I run.
RAE: I don't know about your lumps but your muscles. Whoa. You are buff!
PHOENIX: Fasting. Carb-loading. Vegan dark-earth protein shakes. Want some? So good for you.
RAE: No thanks, I prefer my food pleasurable.
NEL: Pain levels?
PHOENIX: I'm training myself not to feel pain.
RAE: That sounds wise.
NEL: Well, you're ripped. And people are loving it.
RAE: Ooh yes, the Flamers!
PHOENIX: It's wild. They're so ... into me.
RAE: You're allowed to enjoy having fans, Phoenix.
PHOENIX: I remind them to be humbled by the powers, not by me. I am just its vessel.
NEL: And we have to take care of *all* our vessels. Hence our wellness sessions. Rae, back to you.
RAE: Seaweed arms!

They do seaweed arms and continue to follow RAE's *instructions.*

NEL: This is wonderful, thank you, Rae. I had no idea it would be so exhausting.
RAE: People underestimate the demands of public life. They assume it's all luxury and perks.
PHOENIX: It is. You went to Iceland for a sauna. I'm training in Ethiopia.
NEL: We've been working very hard.
PHOENIX: A lot of people work very hard.
RAE: So you've mentioned.
PHOENIX: Just keeping us cognisant of the inherently unfair distribution of wealth and privilege we are operating within and currently benefitting from.

NEL: That's great.

PHOENIX: And I pay for everything. None of that 'celebrities get stuff for free' crap.

RAE: Good for you! Baby roll!

They baby roll.

NEL: I saw that lovely girl who came runner-up, remember her? She was doing a gig at a shopping centre: Super Skillz for Kidz. Very sweet.

RAE: Runners-up often end up doing better than winners on talent shows.

NEL: So true! I've got no idea what the winner is doing. Still keeping whites white I suppose?

PHOENIX: I knew we'd never find anyone that way. True powers are deep and organic.

NEL: Never say never! There are more of us out there somewhere, I just know it.

PHOENIX: It was ridiculous.

RAE: It was perfect. It made us more special, more famous, more money. And we finish with snakeskin slide to thank Mother Earth and honour our timeless power source.

They do snakeskin slide. Perhaps a little liquid spurts or leaks from RAE; *it might smell bad.*

PHOENIX: Whoa. Rae.

NEL: Pee-yew. The leaking is your challenge this week?

RAE: Constant. Even when I'm not crying. It's like a giant tap's been turned on inside me.

NEL: Sealant?

RAE: Helps. It's a bit sticky.

PHOENIX: Stinky.

RAE: It's natural. I'm connecting with my essence.

PHOENIX: You're using a lot of towels. You're using a lot of dark earth protein. Some people don't even have towels.

RAE: Name me one person you know who doesn't have a towel.

NEL: Ladies! This is our scheduled wellness time. We need to take care of ourselves in order to help others. Those with, and those without towels. Agreed? Phoenix. Your turn.

PHOENIX: Alright, gloves off bitches, it's time to get serious.
> *She disrobes and the others follow suit. Some kind of activewear or underwear.*

NEL: Will this be safe for Rae? We don't want her losing too much fluid.
PHOENIX: I had to scream and roll like a baby. She can sweat.
NEL: Rae?
RAE: It's fine, I've got heaps. It's amazing how much fluid the human body contains!
PHOENIX: Let's go!
> PHOENIX *leads them in a workout. It could just be running on the spot or whatever, but a range of activities that are genuinely taxing. The following dialogue runs underneath.*

NEL: By the way I'm fine, thanks both of you for asking.
RAE: How are your headaches, Nel?
NEL: [*putting on giant sunglasses*] These glasses are absolute lifesavers. The tech team are genius. When I put them on I can block out all distractions and my focus improves by exactly four hundred and eighty-eight per cent!
RAE: That's amazing.
PHOENIX: Challenges, Nel?
NEL: None!
PHOENIX: Gratitude?
NEL: Everything! SUPER Corporation is taking off! From grassroots to growth, right here where we started.
PHOENIX: Not really a community space anymore.
NEL: But we are serving the community in so many new ways now! Let's all report on a great win we had during the week!
RAE: That yacht party where I did the cooking demo. I talked about how I went sailing with my dad as a kid, how we could never talk but that was how we bonded. They all started weeping and instantly set up sailing charities for lonely children.
NEL: Incredible!
PHOENIX: Jesus.
RAE: Is the air thin up there on your high horse?
NEL: It's an ecosystem, Phoenix, we all contribute differently. That's what I love about us.

RAE: It was profound.
PHOENIX: What's profound about helping rich people cry?
NEL: Rich people want to cry and feel things. We help them do that.
RAE: I released their deepest desires, their yearning to do something meaningful with their lives.
PHOENIX: To help lonely children sail.
RAE: All children deserve to sail.
PHOENIX: Harder now! Zone Three heart rate. Push push. Zone Four-point-five.
NEL: [*exhausted and struggling*] Phoenix!
PHOENIX: And … done.

   Rae is extremely wet.

NEL: Oh god, Rae.
RAE: I'm a river. It's actually very sensual.
NEL: We'll get some more sealant.
RAE: And look at you, Phoenix, not even puffing.
NEL: [*to* PHOENIX] You are a freak.
PHOENIX: I have to be strong. Because, well, I do have exciting news.
NEL: A win of the week?
PHOENIX: Huge.
NEL: Amazing! What is it?
PHOENIX: During the week, I was contacted, personally, by the head of an amazing refugee charity.
RAE: Ah, the perks of celebrity.
PHOENIX: To do good. But yes. Yes.
NEL: This is such great work validating each other, you two.
PHOENIX: We talked about how I could help kids and families. Defusing anger around them, helping them feel calm. Safe.
NEL: Aha.
PHOENIX: Isn't it awesome!
RAE: It is! And—are they going to pay you?
PHOENIX: Of course not!
NEL: Aha.
RAE: You deserve be paid for your skills.
PHOENIX: This is the kind of work we've been wanting to do.
NEL: Absolutely. And is there a plan—logistics, risk assessment, ethics?
PHOENIX: Well … I mean, we've just started talking.

NEL: Of course, these things aren't ironed out yet.
   Beat.
   This is actually perfect. Symbiotic! Because my win of the week was setting up SUPER as a corporation.
RAE: Wow!
PHOENIX: You did ... that?
NEL: I didn't want to bore you both with the details.
RAE: You superpowered the process.
NEL: Maybe a little. There is so much demand for what we provide, and people are willing to pay. Big bucks. We need a solid financial structure. To ensure sustainable growth.
RAE: Brilliant.
PHOENIX: I don't want to say no to this work.
NEL: No! But what if, hear me out, you could dream ... even bigger.
PHOENIX: Bigger.
NEL: Not just one charity. We leverage. We scale up. We do it our way.
RAE: Money does buy power.
NEL: In fact, Phoenix, you should blue-sky this.
PHOENIX: Blue-sky?
NEL: A proposal. Your proposal. Take the excitement of the charity idea and let it grow. More good.
PHOENIX: To help more people.
NEL: Yes! Everything we used to talk about. Across so many spheres.
PHOENIX: Really?
NEL: Absolutely. We are growing and our profits can pay for pro bono. What do you say?
PHOENIX: Okay. Um. Yes! Blue-sky!
NEL: Amazing! Once we're set up properly, we will be unstoppable. I promise. Oh! One more thing. My wellness contribution. While you were in Iceland, Rae, and Phoenix was doing ultramarathons, I went to a data convention! I got these amazing new data-capture monitor implants. You just stick them on!
   She places some kind of data dot on each of them including herself. Applying them hurts. RAE *gets a little zap.*
RAE: Ouch!
PHOENIX: How is this wellness?

NEL: They send all your stats through to me. No manual reporting! They monitor nutrition, bone density, sleep quality, temperature, bowel movements, everything.
PHOENIX: I don't think I want you knowing when I take a shit?
NEL: Phoenix, we all shared. Mother Earth Therapy is important to Rae, physical workouts are important to you, and data is important to me. It is the answer to our wellness. The data dot, for example, will instantly monitor MHR for your high-altitude-training sessions.
RAE: MHR?
PHOENIX: Maximum Heart Rate.
NEL: See! Super, isn't it.
PHOENIX: Super.
RAE/NEL: Super!
PHOENIX: We are powerful.
NEL: We change the world for good.
RAE: We take huge leaps.
ALL: We never stop.

FOUR

A number of micro-scenes where we see the scale of SUPER Corporation activity, impact and bodily consequences increase at a rapid pace. The overall effect should be like a montage with the characters moving in, through and out of the space quickly in between micro-scenes, even in between lines.

NEL*'s sunglasses are very large.*

NEL: Speed meeting. Super!
ALL: Super!
PHOENIX: We do good at all costs.
RAE: We never say no.
NEL: We adore big data.
ALL: We are amazing!

NEXT.

RAE: I got a fifty-thousand-dollar tip from a real-estate mogul for making him care about architecture again.
NEL: Amazing! But your data dot tells me your water-to-flesh ratio is … soggy. Technical term. The sealant isn't enough. I'll get tech onto it.

NEXT.

> Phoenix, Fast-Food Friday. Calm customers spend more money. On it?

PHOENIX: On it. Did you read my three-pronged proposal? Governance, law and community.

NEL: I will definitely schedule time to review that.

NEXT.

Some kind of inflatable version of PHOENIX *or life-sized cut-out, something to indicate their immensity. It can literally be on stage or they can just reference it.*

RAE: What. Is. That?

NEL: Isn't it fab! Giant Phoenixes everywhere! Merch is next.

NEL *may wear some Phoenix merch at some point.*

NEXT.

NEL: Phoenix, the Calm Queues Beat the Blues Banking Intervention is a hit! Thousands of dropped complaints! The Big Four banks have paid a bonus and booked monthly top-ups.

PHOENIX: Okay. And our meeting? My proposal?

NEL: Diarising it as we speak.

NEXT.

> Rae, your super suit is ready! To keep you completely warm and dry.

This could either be a laborious process we all see, as RAE *squeezed into the suit, or it could be theatre magic and she appears, suddenly suited up.*

PHOENIX: Whoa.

NEXT.

NEL: Challenges?
PHOENIX: Doing more!
RAE: Feeling more!
NEL: Gratitude?
ALL: We're super!

NEXT.

NEL: Phoenix, I secured a militia deal. I don't know who funds them, but all money is good money, right! We're working both sides of the coup. You'll do alternating days until one side runs out of cash.

PHOENIX: When are we meeting to talk?
NEL: Yes!

NEXT.

RAE: What about *my* merch?
NEL: You're exclusive, Rae. Phoenix is our cash cow.

NEXT.

PHOENIX *wearing what could be a complex vest/backpack or simply a few tubes.*

Phoenix, it's a mobile drainage and fluid nutrient pack so you can always be treating your lumps and feeding your muscles. Just don't get the tubes confused or you'll be sucking down your own pus!

NEXT.

Rae, I have you booked for a *Singin' in the Rain* Stadium Spectacular. Go and make it rain!

NEXT.

Phoenix, I've reviewed your ideas.
PHOENIX: Like you said, now we're making real profit. Three prongs where I can have huge impact by stabilising excess emotion. Governance. Law. Community.
NEL: They are very admirable—
PHOENIX: I know.
NEL: And we cannot action any of them. Not even pro bono?
PHOENIX: What? But Parliament. The seat of power.
NEL: Too much paperwork.
PHOENIX: Law enforcement. The arm of power.
NEL: They won't pay.
PHOENIX: Local community. The base of power.
NEL: They can't pay.
PHOENIX: So we're not doing any of them? Not even pro bono?
NEL: No. But thank you for your initiative. It was super.

NEXT.

Rae, how is the suit?
RAE: Fine.
NEL: Staying dry?

RAE: Yes.
NEL: Amazing!
RAE: I don't feel anything.
NEL: But you still cry.
RAE: Yes.
NEL: And others?
RAE: Yes.
NEL: And they do things. Donate. Build. Create.
RAE: Yes.
NEL: Amazing!

NEXT.

Any issues with the data dots, just log a query!

NEXT.

RAE *in her super suit, eating something trashy, maybe a bit weepy.*

NEXT.

PHOENIX *pumping her lumps.*

PHOENIX: I'll just do the real work myself then. The harder I go, the stronger I get. I'm unstoppable.

NEXT.

NEL: Rae, you're getting an amazing sad-girl following.
RAE: I'm not a sad girl, I'm a sad woman!

NEXT.

PHOENIX: I'm sorry I made the loser dudes who don't have superpowers feel like losers.
NEL: That is *not* an apology, Phoenix. It's okay, I've generated one for you and released it to the press.

NEXT.

RAE: I mean I'm just ravenous. All the time. How good is batter!

NEXT.

NEL: Phoenix, your lumps are glowing. They're very pretty but data dots tell me they might be radioactive. I'll get the tech team onto it.

NEXT.

NEL*'s glasses are even bigger, perhaps a full screen or helmet.*
NEL: It's been an incredible quarter, girls. Strongest profit for SUPER Corporation ever. Isn't it amazing?
RAE: Nel!
PHOENIX: Your face!
NEL: Isn't it amazing! Something weird happened to my eyeballs so the tech team made this. The great thing is, it means I never have to switch off. Don't touch me! Super!
ALL: Super! We dominate!

FIVE

RAE *is wet. Her suit half-peeled-off or not on at all. She is relishing fast food. Like the best hangover binge ever.*

PHOENIX *is bloodied, exhausted, exhilarated.*

NEL *is not there.*

RAE: She sent a message: 'Check-in activated. Log queries here. Minimise down time. Exercise peak efficiency. Check-in completed. Super.'
PHOENIX: No. We meet here. In-person check-in. That is what we do.
RAE: I'm here.
PHOENIX: I need access to higher doses of drainage. Only Nel can approve it.
RAE: Log the query, baby!
PHOENIX: I don't want to log a query. She should be here.
  Beat.
What are you eating?
RAE: A Chick-Nugget-Burger-Chip-Feast. It's *so good*. Want some?
PHOENIX: No. You are acting weird, even for you. Are you okay?
RAE: That is so sweet. You know, Phoenix, I really like you.
PHOENIX: Okay.
RAE: In fact, I love you.
PHOENIX: Jesus.
RAE: Not in a superficial 'love you babe!' kind of way. No. I mean real love. I really deeply see you and love you.
PHOENIX: This is making me very uncomfortable.
RAE: Aha! A wise person once said to me things don't have to feel good to be good for us!

PHOENIX: Okay.
RAE: You! You said that!
PHOENIX: I did.
RAE: So let me love you.
PHOENIX: I cannot stop you.
RAE: Also, Phoenix, why are you covered in blood?
PHOENIX: What?

Realises she has some blood on her.

I'm not covered.
RAE: There is quite a lot. Are you menstruating?
PHOENIX: I don't menstruate anymore. High level training.
RAE: Aha. Are you injured? Do you have a clotting issue?
PHOENIX: Nel kept promising. I had a three-pronged proposal. Calm politicians so they make good policy. Dissolve law enforcement and replace it with social care. Defuse community unrest to protect the vulnerable. She wouldn't green-light any of it. So I've been doing it myself. Neighbourhood Watch. Every night.
RAE: But why the blood? Don't you suck anger *out* of situations?
PHOENIX: I'm evolving. I don't just take the violence in now. I can turn it around. It builds so fast. Like tonight. Pack of drunk guys on the prowl. Doesn't take much. 'Hey! Losers!' They come at me—

She acts it out, sucking their anger.

Shunk! Shunk! Shunk! And—

Holds it, power and tension growing, exhilarated.

… BAM! Chuck it straight back at them. They don't stand a fucking chance. There's just so much. So many. Relentless. I can't stop. I can't ever stop. I can't …

RAE *starts to cry. Gently, for real.*

RAE: [*crying*] I'm sorry. I'm not …

PHOENIX *starts to cry. Also gently, for real.*

PHOENIX: [*crying*] It's okay.

They both ease off crying.

RAE: Are you okay?

PHOENIX: Yes.

> *Beat.*
>
> Thank you. That ... helped.
>
> *Beat.*
>
> So yeah. That's why I need higher levels of drainage.

RAE: Hence the query log.
PHOENIX: Fuck the query log.
RAE: Absolutely.
PHOENIX: I mean, Nel should be here in person. Does she even know your suit's not working?
RAE: Oh the suit works fine.
PHOENIX: But you're so ... wet.
RAE: When I wear it I can't feel a thing. But I like to enjoy my Chick-Nugget-Burger-Chip-Feast free as a bird. You like birds, don't you Phoenix? I love that you love birds. I don't know anything about birds. I hate nature. But if you love birds, there must be something amazing about them. Maybe you love me too? I'm sorry—serious, Phoenix—I know this is not your style at all. I get sentimental after my cry parties.
PHOENIX: Your what now?
RAE: Ssh. Don't tell Nel. That's my secret. My sneaky, slippery little late night rendez-vous. Vouses? Anyway, they are very, *very* special.
PHOENIX: Cry parties.
RAE: We get together, whoever comes. Private homes. Very discrete. I start off and then everyone joins in. No stupid waterproof suit. That thing stops me from feeling *anything*. Just people, feeling, together. Life is ... Well. Sometimes we just need to feel sad.
PHOENIX: Yep. We do.
RAE: I really like you, have I told you that?
PHOENIX: You've mentioned it.
RAE: So that's my sneaky secret, Phoenix. I'm a sad, slippery, shimmery little fish.
PHOENIX: Wow. Yep.
RAE: I know you and Nel are thick as thieves so I probably shouldn't have told you.
PHOENIX: No. We're not.

RAE: I've always been a little envious. I don't have friends like that. People don't like me very much. They want things from me, but they don't, like, *like* me.
PHOENIX: I'm sure they do if they get the chance.
RAE: It's okay.
PHOENIX: I ... like you.
RAE: You don't have to say that.
PHOENIX: Anyway, I won't tell Nel about your cry parties.
RAE: And I won't tell her about your vigilante crusades.

Beat.

Challenges?
PHOENIX: Every single thing.
RAE: Gratitude?

Pause.

PHOENIX: I got nothing.

Beat.

We hold our powers with care.
RAE: We strive with short arms.
PHOENIX: Jesus.
RAE: Long arms? All arms!
PHOENIX: We try to make the world a better place. Are we doing that? Are we even close to doing good anymore?
RAE: You've gotta give that shit up. It'll destroy you. Who cares if you're good?
PHOENIX: I care.
RAE: Nup. No point.
PHOENIX: I had a shitty childhood you know, lots of anger. Too much.
RAE: Ah. Your origin story.
PHOENIX: Hm.
RAE: Let me guess, we don't use that term.
PHOENIX: It's very ... (Marvel.)

Beat.

I was messed up. Then Nel spotted me. Made me feel less weird. We did good stuff. Super.
RAE: Birdwatching. By the way—what the hell is a moon bird?

PHOENIX: It's a nickname Nel gave migratory birds. The ones that fly thousands of miles in their lifetime. The distance to the moon. It's absolutely amazing. But it's also just ... what they do.

Beat.

RAE: Tomorrow, I am going to be a fountain at the wedding between the world's two richest oil families.

PHOENIX: I'm booked for staff compliance training at a global pick-and-pack warehouse.

RAE: Calm pick-and-packers are efficient pick-and-packers.

PHOENIX: Yep.

RAE: Oh, I'm still hungry! God, I loved cooking so much. Being with food. And people. Stories and memories. That was all I wanted.

PHOENIX: Your food dream?

RAE: And you said you didn't watch television.

PHOENIX: Once or twice.

Beat.

Friday-night football. Seeing even just one kid. Knowing I'd made their weekend a whole lot better. And now I'm the one ... (being violent.)

RAE: It's different.

PHOENIX: Is it?

Beat.

You should have seen Nel. Flitting around to twenty different community games. Roster in one hand and sauce in the other like a goddamn sausage-sizzle crusader.

RAE: She could take my chutney.

PHOENIX: Your beautiful, weird is-it-sweet-is-it-savoury-what-is-it-anyway chutney.

Beat.

We have to do something.

RAE: Abso-fucking-lutely.

SIX

NEL, PHOENIX *and* RAE.

NEL *may be even more extremely electronic.*

NEL: This is an extraordinary disciplinary-action meeting.
RAE: What?
PHOENIX: This is an intervention.
NEL: What?
RAE: This is a liberation.
PHOENIX: What? Nel, we are worried about you.
NEL: Phoenix, you have abused your superpower in a non-mandated activity that has put the general public at significant risk.
PHOENIX: [*to* RAE] I *knew* I shouldn't have told you anything.
RAE: I didn't! I loved our talk!
NEL: And Rae: 'Sad Sex Parties'?
RAE: [*to* PHOENIX] We bonded!
PHOENIX: Apparently not.
NEL: I thought these were anomalies in the system or periods of intense out-of-hours training, which I appreciated. But once we aggregated the data dot data with circumstantial evidence, I realised the error of my trust in you both. Phoenix, I thought you were just mocking those 'loser dudes', not assaulting them.
PHOENIX: It's your fault for not mandating my three-pronged proposal.
NEL: Oh, live in the real world, Phoenix. Your three prongs were pie in the sky.
PHOENIX: But that was us, Nel! Pies. Skies. Watching for impossible birds. We have to get back to that.
RAE: Exactly!
PHOENIX: Exactly. To return SUPER, and us, to our origins.
RAE: To return to freedom.
PHOENIX: What?
NEL: Your data dot monitoring devices that I have generously kept remote up until now, will from here on in be connected via cables to a centralised processing unit so I can keep tabs on your activities at all times.

RAE: Like lab rats? I am *so* out of here.
PHOENIX: Rae, we agreed we would do something to fix this. Together.

RAE starts to take her suit off.

NEL: Put that back on.
RAE: It's time for me to fly.
NEL: What are you doing? This is not scheduled. This was an extraordinary and undesignated disciplinary session I was forced to convene. Time is money and you are both accruing a second-by-second debt.
PHOENIX: Of course, when the going gets tough Rae gets going.
NEL: Will you stop taking that off? It's time to put it on. Get back to work!
RAE: This can go too! Stupid data dot!

RAE tries to remove her data dot but cannot.

NEL: It's embedded in your skin.
RAE/PHOENIX: What?
NEL: A minor surgery at most, but you don't need to remove it because you're still *at work* on the SUPER Corporation payroll.
PHOENIX: This was never about doing good for you, was it, Rae? You just wanted to feel special in a new way. And Nel, that is a violation of our bodily autonomy.
NEL: Check your contracts, ladies. You agreed to it.
RAE: You couldn't have been *more* thrilled we didn't find any new superpowers. 'Ooh, it's Phoenix saving the world all on her own. One self-righteous neighbourhood attack at a time.'
NEL: This one thing. I made. And grew. For the first time. Real power. You two will *not* destroy it. Rae. Get. Back. Into. Your. Suit.
PHOENIX: At least I'm trying to save the world. All you want is to get people to like you.
RAE: I was very vulnerable when I told you that.

RAE starts to cry.

PHOENIX: [*crying*] Oh that's right, turn on the waterworks. Try to make me feel bad. What a way to always get what you want.
RAE: [*crying*] At least I'm not ashamed of my feelings. You're terrified of them.

SUPER

PHOENIX *works her power on* RAE *who slumps.*
[As if on tranquilisers] See?
NEL: Stop it, you two. Stop it right now!

NEL overrides both other powers and zaps them into extreme acts of administration. Maybe some phones appear.

PHOENIX: Agh! She's making me sync my calendar.

A stack of filing magically appears.

RAE: This filing isn't going to file itself!
PHOENIX: You know it really *does* make a lot more sense to have a password manager than just add an exclamation mark and year to each password.
NEL: All freedoms curbed from now on. You will commence central processing unit data cable connectivity immediately.

NEL might have some cables she is trying to hook them up with. RAE and PHOENIX use their powers to struggle against NEL. RAE is making them cry. PHOENIX *is making them numb.* NEL *is forcing administrative tasks. They keep flipping between the states throughout the following dialogue:*

PHOENIX: I don't want to do it. I hate password managers! I hate being connected. And I hate crying.
NEL: The Harvard Business School Online says there are six primary reasons why a manager or leader might be reluctant to delegate.
RAE: I have to live my bliss!
NEL: Systems connecting. Saving automatically to the drive.
PHOENIX: You're just jealous because you've never had friends.
RAE: That is a low blow.
NEL: Always deliver, always be improving. Deliver more and your customer will hit the ceiling. Beat emotion with data. Chase the first version of your own skin, don't tip off competitors.
PHOENIX: That doesn't even make any sense.
RAE: Data doesn't lie. I am ones and zeros, and all information is stored forever.
NEL: We started the fire and your gasoline is a never-ending stream the appointments can't wait the demand.
RAE: I'm flying away. Am I? Do I even care. What are wings?

PHOENIX: You can't leave! Look at her!
RAE: I don't know how to help her. I've never known how to help anyone.
PHOENIX: None of us do. The point is we try.
NEL: Our work approach and priority is to save your work make work the working work of the working group.
RAE: Is the three of us here really the most efficient rostering solution?
NEL: Don't touch me. The data dots make an electrical current.
PHOENIX: Let. Me. Help. You.
NEL: The data dots!
RAE: This. Is. All. Very. Challenging.

> PHOENIX *lays her hands on* NEL *and* NEL *starts sparking.*

NEL: ... d-d-d-d— ... c-c-c-c-c-c ...
RAE: Oh my god, she's on fire.
PHOENIX: Stupid goddamn da-da-da-da ...

> PHOENIX *is also sparking.*

RAE: Nel! Phoenix!

> RAE *reaches out to* NEL *and* PHOENIX *tries to stop her.*
>
> *They are all connected, sparking, current charging through them.*

PHOENIX: Rae, s-s-s-top crying! Water. Electricity.
RAE: I can't! It's out of my control.
NEL: Work is beautiful. Work. Wrk. Wrrrrrrrrk. Wrrrrrrr.

> *Surge.*
>
> *Power blackout.*

SEVEN

RAE *may be dripping into a bucket.*

PHOENIX*'s lumps gradually lose their glow.*

NEL *is wearing large sunglasses.*

Time starts to behave strangely in this scene. As it progresses, the characters lose their sense of who they are, their powers and their relationship to each other.

PHOENIX: [*trying to start the check-in*] Super!
NEL: No.

Beat.

RAE: Lemon Zest Snap?

Beat.

PHOENIX: How are everybody's singe marks?

RAE: Sore! Helping people hurts.

Beat.

PHOENIX: Nel. Say something. Please.

NEL: I am never forgiving either of you.

Beat.

RAE: It could be worse.

NEL: We destroyed a building and blacked out the city. I don't know yet where we stand legally and financially. The data breaches of highly sensitive information were astronomical. We might be facing criminal charges. But more than that, you two colluded, betrayed and attacked me. I *told* you not to touch me.

PHOENIX: It was those stupid dots. Data was literally going to kill us.

NEL: It was you disobeying me.

RAE: At least the stupid dots fell out when everything short-circuited.

Beat.

I'm grateful for that.

NEL: Everything we worked for. Ruined. The utter selfishness.

Beat.

RAE: This will blow over. We're today's news for a minute and then, we won't be. Celebrity cycle, believe me, I know.

PHOENIX *eats a Lemon Zest Snap.*

PHOENIX: Wow. These are delicious.

RAE: I know.

PHOENIX: Nel?

NEL *refuses.*

I've drawn up a few safeguard parameters. Nel, you're the admin queen, could you take a look?

NEL: There's no point.

PHOENIX: Shall we start a proper clean-up? It's getting pretty dank in here.

NEL: To clean up would imply there is something worth cleaning up for.

Beat.

There are just so many people to help.

Beat.

They weren't even grateful.

Beat.

RAE: [*trying to start the check-in*] Super!
NEL: No.

Beat.

RAE: I respect that you're not ready yet, Nel, but I am going to start anyway. I'm Rae. I acknowledge that I used my power and inadvertently electrocuted my colleagues and caused a sprinkler-system incident and minor flood. I acknowledge the harm I did. I am sorry for hurt that I caused. And I am amending by avoiding situations where I might cry or bring about inappropriate episodes of crying in others. Phoenix?
PHOENIX: I'm Phoenix and I acknowledge that I take a lot of pleasure from sucking anger out of packs of dickheads and hurling it back at them.
RAE: O … kay. Interesting first try. Anything else?
PHOENIX: I am sorry for the limbs I broke.
RAE: And you are amending by …
PHOENIX: Not breaking any more limbs.
RAE: And, Phoenix, what constructive activities are you engaging with to give your powers time to rest? For example, I am masturbating.
PHOENIX: Ha.
RAE: A lot. It's not very satisfying. But I'm trying. So?
PHOENIX: Nothing. I'm doing nothing. I was occasionally punching my lumps to reduce them. But that hurt.
RAE: Maybe you could try punching a pillow? We don't have to change who we are, Phoenix. Our aim is to know ourselves better so we can avoid causing harm to our self and others.
PHOENIX: I am not going to punch a pillow.

Beat.

NEL: Have you tried pornography?
PHOENIX: What?
NEL: Rae.
RAE: Yes.
NEL: Which—
RAE: All of it. Like I said, not very satisfying. I mean nothing, *nothing* comes close to …
PHOENIX: That beautiful wave.
RAE: That magical wave.

Beat.

PHOENIX: They never have to do this in the movies.
RAE: Who?
PHOENIX: Superheroes. Those guys tear up entire worlds. Mass destruction. They just skulk back to their planets or lairs or whatever then come back to swing their dicks around another day.
RAE: They're not real, Phoenix.
PHOENIX: I know.
NEL: Superheroes.
PHOENIX: I know!
NEL: No. Not them. Us. You called us superheroes. Kind of.
PHOENIX: Yeah. Well. We are. The world needs us.
NEL: How are your lumps?
PHOENIX: Almost gone.
NEL: Rae?
RAE: Just about dried up. A few drips now and then.
PHOENIX: Your eyes, Nel?
NEL: Nearly back to normal.

NEL *takes her sunglasses off.*

I'm Nel. I acknowledge that my love of spreadsheets got a little out of control.
RAE/PHOENIX: Hi Nel.
NEL: I am meditating on impermanence and the truth that I don't have to be organising things or being helpful in order to have value as a person. My value is inherent, and I can do … nothing and still … mean something.
PHOENIX: Whoa.

RAE: Well done, Nel.

   Beat.

NEL: Thelma.

PHOENIX: What about her?

NEL: I think something similar happened to her. Powers getting out of control. She started getting overwhelmed, saying she could hear everything, from everywhere. Too much. Like a radio she couldn't turn off. She tried to tell me. But I didn't listen. Her powers. I think they might have killed her.

RAE: Oh, Nel.

NEL: I could have helped, but I didn't.

PHOENIX: Wasn't she like … eighty-six?

NEL: Are you saying it's not sad when old people die?

PHOENIX: I just mean she lived a good, long life.

NEL: Do you want me to be sad when you die?

PHOENIX: That won't happen again. We'll look out for each other.

NEL: No need. I'm done.

PHOENIX: You just need a break.

RAE: The guidelines—if we don't use the powers, we'll forget we have them?

PHOENIX: That is not happening to us. We reset. Go back to how it was. Just us three, no company, just us. Doing our thing.

RAE: Three.

PHOENIX: Yes.

   Beat.

You were right, Nel. We found one more. And I didn't hate it. In the end.

NEL: I can't risk anything like that again. We messed up.

RAE: Yep.

PHOENIX: All of us.

   From here, time starts to warp and leapfrog.

   NEXT.

   RAE *has a container of slice.*

RAE: I made slice. Lemon.

NEL: Delicious.

PHOENIX *tries some.*

PHOENIX: Mm. Thanks, Rae.

NEXT.

If you're going to stop, I will too.

NEL: No! It's my decision.

RAE: One in, all in.

PHOENIX: No, we're *stopping.*

RAE: One out, all out.

PHOENIX: That sounds weird.

RAE: You really have to criticise every single thing I say.

NEL: Ladies!

NEXT.

RAE: Okay! We covered some good ground today. Nice sharing everyone.

PHOENIX: I'd better get to work. Had I? Do I work? I mean, of course I ... I mean. Our roster. What are we up to, Nel? Local sports clubs?

NEL: [*savouring the slice*] Ooh did you make this slice, Rae? It's amazing.

RAE: Yes! I'm trying something new. Lemon zest.

NEXT.

PHOENIX: Good session today.

NEL: Your glow. Phoenix, it's nearly out.

RAE: The dripping. Remember there was something dripping? I was wet. I think. Anyway, it's stopped.

PHOENIX: I almost forgot the way here today. Isn't that stupid?

RAE: As long as we have each other. Sort of like a buddy system.

PHOENIX: Yeah.

NEL: Looking out for each other.

NEXT.

PHOENIX: I don't want to not know you two.

NEL: What a funny thing to say.

RAE: I never thought I'd be part of anything like this.

PHOENIX: Motherfucking superheroes.

RAE: I mean friends. I've never had friends like you two.

NEXT.

NEL: It's dark. Is it getting dark?
RAE: Little bit of water spilled here. I wonder if there's a mop?
NEL: They were so pretty. The lights.
PHOENIX: I guess there's a switch here somewhere. Power box. Something.

NEXT.

RAE *might be mopping.* PHOENIX *looking for a light switch.*

There we go.
RAE: Nice one. How many are we expecting, do you think?
PHOENIX: Dunno. I only just started coming. I mean, I've been here for ages. Or. I've been waiting. I think. For.

RAE *has a lemon and a zester.*

RAE: Well, I brought these! I guess I was going to make something.
NEL: Delicious! It's such a busy time of year. Thanks all for coming. Shall we get started? I'm Nel and I ... um, well, it's hard to remember exactly why I started coming but I think, I try to control situations sometimes, make everything happen my way. And that can be ... yeah.
PHOENIX/RAE: Hi Nel.
PHOENIX: I'm Phoenix. I get really overwhelmed. Especially by anger. And it makes me ... angry.
NEL/RAE: Hi Phoenix.
RAE: I'm Rae. I've been feeling irrelevant.
NEL/PHOENIX: Hi Rae.
NEL: Rae, have we met? You look familiar.
RAE: I hate saying this as it sounds so pompous, but I did used to have a TV cooking show and some people know me from that.
NEL: Of course! That was a great show. Is it still on?
RAE: Yes.
NEL: Exciting!
RAE: But I'm no longer on it. It happens suddenly, by surprise. A meeting you thought would go one way, you had it all planned, this new show, chutney, new ideas, and that's all they say: 'We're going in a different direction this time, Rae.' Just like that.
PHOENIX: Rough.
RAE: I started crying and it feels like ... I can't stop. My doctor thinks it might be hormonal.

PHOENIX: Or completely justifiable anger at losing your job.
NEL: It's very difficult, the feeling of being replaced. You'll find something else.
RAE: I don't know.
NEL: Just pick one thing and do it well. That's what my gran said. Or was it someone famous? Gandhi? Anyway, you can't save the whole world. Just do what you can. Each day.
PHOENIX: That's always been my approach. A lot of people depend on me doing my very best every day.
RAE: That's marvellous. I'm envious.
PHOENIX: Joke. I'm joking. I work in a car park.
NEL: People need to park their cars.
PHOENIX: What they mostly need is help operating the ticket machine.

RAE holds the lemon and the zester. She looks confused.

RAE: I brought these.

NEXT.

Are we waiting for any others?
NEL: I think we might be it. Just the three of us.
PHOENIX: Remember Thelma?
NEL: Yes. Lovely Thelma.
RAE: It's damp in here, isn't it? Water damage of some kind? I was looking for a mop.
PHOENIX: Dark, too. Light falls away so fast this time of year.
NEL: Now, Phoenix, is it you who loves birds?
PHOENIX: Yeah. That's so sweet of you to remember.
NEL: Because I saw this beautiful video the other day, of birds flying all together in formation. What do they call that?
PHOENIX: A murmuration. Starlings.
NEL: Murmuration! Lovely!
PHOENIX: Swarm intelligence. Like ants and bees—the collective as a whole is smarter, better for survival than each individual functioning alone. And, um, you're ... into running, right?
NEL: Ah, I want to be! I don't know where to start.
PHOENIX: I can help with that.
RAE: I think I've got it all. It's hard to see, so be careful both of you, I don't want you to slip.

PHOENIX: We could develop some guidelines for the group. And a name maybe, or a motto, something cute.
NEL: Now, let me make everyone a nice cup of tea. We only have Lipton's, I'm afraid. Nothing fancy.

A little magical sting. The tea appears very quickly.

PHOENIX: Wow, that was quick.
RAE: Almost like a superpower.
NEL: Oh no, it was nothing!
RAE: Oh, look! I've brought … biscuits.

Something very ordinary.

NEL: Thank you! I only brought some now-cold chips from the takeaway.
RAE: I like cold chips. They remind me of late nights, hangovers, bad sex.
PHOENIX: These biccies remind me of being a kid. My mum used to get them for cheer-ups. I haven't thought about them in years.
NEL: Delicious, thank you, Rae! Such a pretty word, murmuration. Do they actually murmur, the birds? Or is that just a saying? Because it would sound beautiful, wouldn't it? Flying all together. Murmuring. Like a hum. Anyway, enough of my prattling. Let's get on.
PHOENIX: Did you hear—?
RAE: Hello? Is someone there?
NEL: Come on in! We're just about to begin.

THE END

presents

Super

11 JUNE - 6 JULY, 2025

Playwright
Emilie Collyer

Director/Dramaturg
Emma Valente

Set and Costume Design
Romanie Harper

Lighting Design
Natalia Velasco Moreno

Sound Design
Beau Esposito

Associate Director
Cassandra Fumi

Assistant Set and Costume Design
Dylan Lumsden

Stage Manager
Ellen Perriment

Assistant Stage Manager
Kara Floyd

Phoenix – **Lucy Ansell**
Rae – **Caroline Lee**
Nel – **Laila Thaker**

This play was developed through Red Stitch's INK writing program.

Red Stitch — THE ACTORS' THEATRE

Established in 2001, Red Stitch is Australia's leading acting ensemble.

Our home space of 80 seats in St Kilda has produced critically lauded theatre for 24 years, with over 175 productions to our name, contributing to our reputation as a leading commissioner and producer of exceptional Australian theatre. Our INK program sustains the increased representation of Australian drama in the national repertoire, supporting an illustrious coalition of playwrights and artists. Nineteen Australian plays have been produced, one third of which have toured nationally or internationally. Our biennial site-specific festival of music and new writing, PLAYlist, has attracted a large and loyal audience and a vibrant reputation in the community.

Our determination to create a pathway for emerging artists to traverse the challenging transition from tertiary institutions to the professional sector led the company to establish the Red Stitch Graduate program in 2008. Today the Hansen Graduate Program supports five early career practitioners annually, offering young artists the opportunity to work with the company throughout the year across a range of disciplines gaining vital hands-on experience. This has in turn furnished the company with fresh perspectives and ideas.

Current Artistic Director/CEO, Ella Caldwell, oversees a company in which over 60 artists have occupied ensemble positions, with 12-15 advisors active at any time and membership refreshed annually. Several original ensemble members hold advisory positions and regularly return to work with the company along with guest artists who bring their vision, talent and energy to the company.

Red Stitch is a resilient, constantly evolving and uniquely creative company, earning recognition and awards alongside much better funded high profile counterparts. As a crucial bridge between independent practice and larger institutions, our artists evolve and hone their craft while simultaneously generating exceptional work for audiences.

Red Stitch has earned a treasured place in the theatre-going community of Melbourne and contributed significantly to the national culture.

Thank you for joining us.

Artistic Director/CEO
Ella Caldwell

Production and Technical Manager
Charlie Bowyer

Front-of-House Manager
Penelope Thomson

Producer
Krystalla Pearce

Marketing Coordinator
Darcy Kent

Finance Manager
Shadi Habash

RED STITCH ENSEMBLE

Lucy Ansell	Darcy Kent
Jacob Battista	Caroline Lee
Ella Caldwell	Olga Makeeva
Richard Cawthorne	Dion Mills
Jing-Xuan Chan	Christina O'Neil
Jessica Clarke	Tim Potter
Kate Cole	Ben Prendergast
Brett Cousins	Kat Stewart
Ngaire Dawn Fair	Sarah Sutherland
Daniel Frederikson	Andrea Swifte
Emily Goddard	David Whiteley
Kevin Hofbauer	Sophie Woodward
Justin Hosking	Harvey Zielinski
Khisraw Jones-Shukoor	

BOARD

Humphery Clegg (Chair), Stephen Sweeney (Treasurer), Melanie Sherrin (Secretary), Ella Caldwell, Jing-Xuan Chan, Andrew Domasevicius-Zilinskas, Sam Frey, Khisraw Jones-Shukoor, Belinda Locke, Joanna Murray-Smith and Michael Rich.

We at Red Stitch acknowledge and pay our respects to Australia's First Peoples and Elders past and present, and offer our gratitude to the Boon Wurrung and Wurundjeri Woi Wurrung peoples of the Kulin Nation, on whose unceded lands we work.

THANK YOU

This development and production of *Super* would not have been possible without the generous support of our donors and partners

KINDRED DONORS

Ms Jane Hansen AO
Maureen Wheeler AO & Tony Wheeler AO
Jane & Stephen Hains & Portland House Foundation
Andrew Domasevicius SLD & Aida Tuciute
Carrillo Gantner AC & ZiYin Gantner AC
Peter Bartholomew
Beecher Family Charitable Trust, a Sub-Fund of the Australian Communities Foundation
Per & Ingrid Carlsen
Sage Custodians
Graham & Judy Hubbard
Brenda Joyce
Myer Foundation
Anonymous
Anthony Adair
Beth Brown
The Eric and Elizabeth Gross Foundation
Joanna Murray-Smith AO
The Neff Family
Jenny Schwarz In Memoriam
KSS Foundation
Rosemary Walls
Diana Burleigh
Coote Family Lawyers
Anthony & Susan Dickinson
Michael Kingston
Halina Lewenberg Charitable Foundation
Kate Langbroek on behalf of The Lewis Langbroek Charitable Endowment
Mark O'Dwyer
Craig Reeves
Fiona Symonds
Richard Brettell & Robyn Trevaskis
Christine Turner
Margaret & Peter Yuill
Larry Abel
Anonymous
APS Foundation
Anita & Graham Anderson
Ella Caldwell
Robin Carter

Julie & Ian Cattlin
Richard Dammery
Edwina Mary Lampitt in Memoriam
Damon & Lorena Healey
Linda Herd
Tony Hillery
Akhilesh Jain
Dr George Klempfner
KCL Law
Barbara Long
Lyngala Foundation
Lousie Manson
Patricia Mason
Angela & Peter Matkovic
Kaylene O'Neil
Donna Pelka
Timothy Roman
Victoria Rowell
Jenny Ryssenbeek
Simon Schofield
Marshall Segan
James H Syme
Jane Thompson
Peter Veevers & Jenny Veevers
Tony War & Gail Ryan
Graham Webster & Teri Snowdon
Jane Whiting AM

MAJOR PARTNERS
Creative Victoria
Cybec Foundation
City of Port Phillip
Malcolm Robertson Foundation
The Myer Foundation
Sidney Myer Fund
Copyright Agency Cultural Fund
Lyngala Foundation
Playking Foundation
Seaborn, Broughton & Walford Foundation

Rear 2 Chapel Street, St Kilda East, VIC 3183
http://redstitch.net/ | FB: @RedStitchTheatre | T: @redstitch
boxoffice@redstitch.net | 03 9533 8083

PLAYWRIGHT'S NOTES

'I love going to plays. There's a subconscious side to it, obviously—some people like to be spanked for XYZ psychological reasons, and I like to go to plays, and I can't entirely explain Why.'

I have this quote from a Paris Review interview with Wallace Shawn pinned above my desk. I'd say the same for writing plays —it's subconscious, kind of like a spanking, I love it (and hate it at times, it's impossible and frustrating) and I can't exactly explain why. As for putting plays on, it takes villages, mountain movers and miracles.

I first conceptualised *Super* in 2017. I'd just finished a year of treatment for breast cancer, during which time I'd had no desire or energy for writing. I had wondered if that might be it.

Then, tendrils of an idea started to furl. A woman goes to a medical facility because she can't stop crying, and she meets a person who believes she has superpowers. That was it. An image, a feeling, a situation. Looking back, I can see that while I wasn't writing a 'cancer play', I was writing something about my experience with cancer, with the medical system, with the profound and visceral reminder of the vulnerability of our bodies. This was the seed and, via writing, developing and questioning, other ideas emerged: about the pressures on bodies within a capitalist economic system where value is based on productivity; about the very real urge most of us have to 'do good'; about how this urge also gets siphoned into mechanisms of wealth and influence; about the connections between an endless growth mindset and cells wildly proliferating; about our deeply human desire to control things, including our own bodies, that are beyond our control; and about superheroes – who they are and what kinds of powers get to be called super.

This play took time. I completed an entire PhD while *Super* has been in development. Many of the ideas from the play fed into my research (about the value of feminist creative practice and how we measure notions of failure and success) and vice versa. I nearly gave up on the play a few times. In among the ideas, I just couldn't find its heart. But something kept pulling at me and fortunately I had some remarkable people around who quietly believed in the work and had the patience and skill to help me discover what the play wanted to be.

So, now, after many years of writing and re-writing, what is *Super*? Is it, as many people have inquired upon hearing its title, a play about superannuation? Well, no. Although it is a little bit about how we try and shore up our lives for the future. Sitting underneath are all of the strange, quite dark, visceral memories of cancer diagnosis and treatment that birthed it.

Woven through are my big questions about care and compassion, exploitation and fatigue. What has surprised and delighted me is that the play really is about the (super) power of friendship and how this sustains us through all of life's bonkers ups and downs. I want the play to take audiences on an absurd and not-quite-sensical ride, to make them laugh and perhaps feel a few other things too. While it won't be at all like watching a Marvel movie, it will be something parallel; perfect for those who love a bit of superpower schtick and equally for those who don't. A kind of loving, skewering homage. I think maybe it's also just a bit weird and that's okay too. Something that came from deep within me and has found a form that is shareable with others. XYZ. Spank, spank.

Super has had so many incredible people contribute to its development. Luke Kerridge and Maude Davey were both attached as directors at different times throughout the play's long gestation and contributed marvellous and vital dramaturgical wisdom. Thanks to the many actors who have been in the room over the years, every one of whom helped shape the characters and nut out the story and the world as it kept morphing and shifting. These include (and I apologise to anyone I have missed due to my own poor memory) Olivia Monticciolo, Katherine Tonkin, Ben Pfeiffer, Harvey Zielinski, Christina O'Neill, Olga Makeeva, Kevin Hofbauer, Jing-Xuan Chan, Shontane Farmer, Emily Goddard and our current beautiful, absolutely super cast Caroline Lee, Laila Thaker and Lucy Ansell. Special thanks to Caroline for penning a beautiful introduction to the script. Some dear friends and brilliant theatre minds gave feedback along the way, including Petra Kalive, Michele Lee, Emily

Sheehan and Mark Wilson, as well as my partner Ross, who has given constant counsel in hundreds of spontaneous 'how do superpowers work in this world' conversations and talked me down from multiple 'I can't fix this I have no idea what to do next' ledges. I thank my stars and pinch myself regularly at the fortune of working with director and dramaturg Emma Valente. Life changing. And the phenomenal creative team bringing *Super* to life (and my apologies for some of the ridiculous design challenges I've created): associate director Cassandra Fumi, set and costume designer Romanie Harper, lighting designer Natalia Velasco Moreno, sound designer Beau Esposito, set and costume assistant Dylan Lumsden, stage manager Ellen Perriment and assistant stage manager Kara Floyd.

I am grateful for support from Melbourne Theatre Company for a day's development on the script in its infancy. The work has also been supported by funding from Australian Plays Transform Duologue program and the Besen Family Foundation. The script was shortlisted for the Queensland Premier's Drama Award.

My huge thanks to Red Stitch for commissioning this play via their brilliant INK program and to the ensemble for supporting the work. Particular heartfelt thanks to Ella Caldwell for believing in Super and in me over such a long period and shepherding us through various challenges (including a pandemic and an ever-constricting arts funding environment) to get the play on. I never take these opportunities for granted. I know how much hard work and labour goes into nurturing new writing for the stage and keeping the lights on at any theatre company. Respect and gratitude to you all for moving mountains on the regular.

Emilie Collyer
Playwright

ACTOR'S NOTES

What is a play? In the widest possible terms a play is a piece of writing, which is performed in a theatre. A play begins its creation in the imagination of the writer, from nothing, from air, from an image, a character, a theme, an idea, a thought, a sentence. These elements multiply, they grow, they take shape, they connect into a story; a story which exists as marks on a page (the script) but which suggests, provokes, and invokes a three-dimensional form, as well as having a crucial relationship to the fourth dimension, time, both in creation and performance.

The creation of *Super* by Emilie Collyer has taken time. We did the first reading of the first draft in August 2018. It takes considerable time to craft and shape a new work, particularly a work which is as original and unusual as *Super*. We have been fortunate that the structure of the development process for Red Stitch INK plays (new Australian plays) is flexible enough to allow this time. Time for workshopping with actors; analysis; discussions between writer, director and designer; a reading of the work to a small audience; and most importantly thinking time: time for the writer to consider, process, and to carefully shape and hone the work.

And now this beautiful work has arrived. An absurdist, anti-capitalist, dark comedy. *Super* is, on the page, a deceptively straightforward story of three women with very specific (super) powers who allow those powers to become monetised, and as a result corrupted, leading to disaster. Yet it is much more than that. The three-dimensional performed version of the play has many layers of meaning and association, amongst which are: super hero comics and films; feminist theory; capitalist theory; absurdist theatre; analysis of colonialism; the corporatisation of medical care; and Pop Art. These references and influences float under, and drift through, the work making it a complex, exciting, living, multi-dimensional creation. Over the past six and half years, it has been a joy to be involved in the making of this work and its world. From the lightest breath of air to *Super*.

Caroline Lee
Actor

EMILIE COLLYER
PLAYWRIGHT

Emilie Collyer is an award-winning playwright and poet. Her writing has been published in *Meanjin, Overland, Griffith Review, Island* and *Kill Your Darlings* among many others. Her poetry collection *Do you have anything less domestic?* (Vagabond Press 2022) won the inaugural Five Islands Prize and she has been runner up in the Gwen Harwood Poetry Prize and shortlisted in the Newcastle Poetry Prize. Her writing credits for theatre include *Argonauta, Promise, The Good Girl, Once Were Pirates, Dream Home, Contest* and *Super*, produced in Australia, New York, Los Angeles, Edinburgh and Prague. She has been commissioned by many of Australia's leading theatre companies including Melbourne Theatre Company, Malthouse Theatre, Red Stitch Theatre and The Street Theatre. Her plays have won and been nominated for multiple awards including Theatre503 International Playwriting Award (London), Queensland Premier's Drama Award, Green Room Association Awards, George Fairfax Prize, Patrick White Playwriting Award (twice nominated) and the Malcolm Robertson Prize. Emilie has a PhD in Creative Writing from RMIT.

EMMA VALENTE
DIRECTOR/DRAMATURG

Emma Valente is a freelance director, dramaturg, lighting designer and occasional trouble maker. She is the Co Artistic director and Co CEO of feminist theatre company THE RABBLE. Emma is the recipient of the Creators Fund grant from Creative Victoria, a Sidney Myer Fellow, a Curator at Large (performance) at The SUBSTATION and received a Life Time Achievement award for Technical Achievement from The Green Room Awards. Emma has directed works that have been performed at Red Stitch, Malthouse Theatre, PICA, Arts Emerson(Boston), Noorderzon Festival (Groningen),

Dar es Salaam Little Theatre, OzAsia Festival, iBox Theatre (Penang), Box Office Theatre (Phnom Penh), Arts Centre Melbourne, Colgate University (New York), Puebla City Theatre, Adolfo Llauradó Theatre (Havana) Berlin Theatertreffen, Dublin Fringe Festival, Wuzhen Festival (China), Vitalstatistix, Arts House, St Martins, Melbourne International Arts Festival, Dark MOFO, Brisbane Festival, Belvoir Theatre, MTC, The Substation, Theatre Works, CarriageWorks and La Mama. Emma has been the dramaturg for artists including Nicola Gunn, Wang Chong, Liv Satchell, Eryn Jean Norvill, Emma McManus, Rachel Perks, Alison Croggon, Angus Cerini, Zoey Dawson, Bridget Mackey, Daniel Schlusser, Andrea James, Elise Hearst and Meg Wilson. Emma's essay on Dramaturgy and Silence was published by the centre for Dramaturgy and Curation. Emma is also an award-winning Lighting Design and has worked for many major theatre companies across the country.

ROMANIE HARPER
SET AND COSTUME DESIGN

Romanie Harper is a designer from Naarm/Melbourne working across theatre, dance and experimental performance. Recent design credits include *The Black Woman of Gippsland, Meet Me at Dawn* and *Sunshine Super Girl* (Melbourne Theatre Company), *Swim* (Griffin Theatre Company), *Fu*ck Christmas, Nosferatu, K-BOX, Australian Realness, Trustees, Good Muslim Boy* and *Little Emperors* (Malthouse), *8/8/8: REST* and *8/8/8:WORK* (Rising Festival), *The Crying Room; Exhumed* (The Substation), *The Master & Margarita, The Cherry Orchard* and *Packer and Sons* (Belvoir St Theatre), *Shhh* and *Desert 6.29pm* (Red Stitch Actors Theatre), *Hercules, Die! Old People Die!* and *We All Know Whats Happening* (Arts House), *What Am I Supposed to Do?* (Deep Souful Sweats), *Slip, Contest* and *Moral Panic* (Darebin Speakeasy), *Bad Boy, Runt* and *This Is Eden* (Fortyfive Downstairs).

NATALIA VELASCO MORENO
LIGHTING DESIGN

Natalia brings over a decade of lighting design experience, spanning architecture, film, and theatre. Her portfolio encompasses projects in museums, galleries, and public spaces across Australia and overseas, as well as contributions to international cinematic productions, television, and independent theatre. Combining experience as a technician, rigger, and draftsperson, and having a background in art and painting, Natalia is driven by her passion for crafting immersive experiences through colour and form. Her primary focus lies in contemporary performance lighting, where she is interested in combining artistic expression with technical precision to bring narratives to life.

BEAU ESPOSITO
SOUND DESIGN

Beau is a trans masculine composer and sound designer from Naarm, working across theatre and film. He is a graduate of Victorian College of the Arts and holds a Bachelor of Fine Arts in Production. Beau's credits include sound design and composition for: *The Sound Inside* (Melbourne Theatre Company); *Sex Magick* (Griffin Theatre); *Telethon Kid* (Malthouse Theatre) *Stay Woke* (Malthouse/ Darlinghurst Theatre Company); *Overflow* (Darlinghurst Theatre Company); *Hydra* (Darebin Arts); *Darkness* (NewTheatricals); *Cavemxn* (Anthropocene Play Company); *Winter Feast, Night Mass* (Dark Mofo); *Fast Food* (Red Stitch); *Slutnik, Guerilla Sabbath, Adam* (Midsumma Festival); *Cactus* (La Mama); *Punk Rock* (Patalog Theatre); *Slut* (The Burrow); *The Dream Laboratory* (Essential Theatre); *Girl at the Bottom of the Well* (A Ry Presentation); *Treats* and *Brittany and the Mannequins* (Fever103 Theatre); *Land* (Three Fates Theatre Company); *Never Said Motel* (Melbourne Writers Festival); *Tram Lights Up* (Bighouse Arts). Beau was associate sound designer for Sunday with MTC. Beau was nominated for a Green Room Award for their work on Hydra and for a Sydney Theatre Award for their work on *Overflow* and *Sex Magick*. Beau was a panel member for the Green Rooms, 2022, Theatre Companies.

CASSANDRA FUMI
ASSOCIATE DIRECTOR

Cassandra Fumi is an award winning theatre director. Directing credits include; *Rhinoceros* (fortyfivedownstiars), *World Problems* (Melbourne Theatre Company), *The Crocodile* (Winner Best Director 2024 Green Room Awards), *Far Away* (fortyfivedownstiars), *The Mermaid* (La Mama Theatre - 2021 VCE Playlist), *Dog Show* (Melbourne Fringe Hub). She was the Associate Director on *A Very Jewish Christmas Carol* (Melbourne Theatre Company) and Assistant Director on *The House of Bernarda Alba* (Melbourne Theatre Company). She has a longstanding collaboration with The Rabble as Stage Manager on *Lone, Unwoman, Yes* and Community Liaison for *Wake*. Cassandra is the Associate Artist on *Body Of Knowledge* with Samara Hersch. Cassandra loves the way theatre can break down barriers, form community and allow for a group of people to work towards a creative goal collectively. www.cassandrafumi.com

DYLAN LUMSDEN
ASSISTANT SET AND COSTUME DESIGN

Dylan is a Melbourne-based Set & Costume Designer who recently graduated with a Bachelor of Fine Arts (Production) from the Victorian College of the Arts. Dylan is inspired to create imaginative and impactful scenographic work that visually captivates audiences through meaningful creative collaborations. While at VCA Dylan also specialised in Costume Management and Construction. Dylan's credits include Costume

Designer for *A Very Expensive Poison*, Assistant Costume Designer for *BORNEO plus 3*, Costume Manager for the VCA choreographic dance production *before, between, beyond* and Senior Costumier on *Spring Awakening*. You can view Dylan's work at dylanlumsden.com

ELLEN PERRIMENT
STAGE MANAGER

Ellen Perriment (they/she) is a stage manager and theatre technician based in Naarm. Their best-known work includes stage management and operation for *DJUNA* with Bullet Heart Club, stage and technical management for Frankie Van Kan's *A Body at Work* and stage management for *Le Freak* (Theme Fatale and Elle Diablo). Having undertaken a Diploma of Live Production and Technical Services at RMIT in 2024, a Bachelor of Arts at Monash University in 2017, and working in theatre front of house through 2022, they bring a socially conscious, technically informed, and practical approach to all their work. Ellen has been an operator and stage manager as part of the Adelaide Fringe Festival, Melbourne Fringe Festival, Midsumma Festival, and Melbourne International Comedy Festival, toured nationally with the burlesque troupe *The Sugar Showgirls*, and currently work in freelance technical services across the country. Ellen is also a passionate educator, delivering workshops and one-on-one sessions on the fundamentals of technical production for at performing artists, and are a proud MEAA member since 2024.

KARA FLOYD
ASSISTANT STAGE MANAGER

Kara Floyd is a Naarm based stage manager originally from Townsville, North Queensland. She is currently completing her Bachelor of Stage Management at The Australian College of the Arts and works with both the theatre and in the circus. Her best-known works are *Small Acts of Resistance* with The Women's Circus (2025), *Eigengrau* with The Beehive Players (2025), and Burning

House's *Cymbeline* (2024) as assistant stage manager and costume designer, as well as works for Melbourne Fringe and operating for The Motley Bauhaus. Kara is dedicated to bringing technical knowledge and professionalism to every space. She is excited to further her career in stage management and technical operation, as well as furthering her knowledge of costume design and construction. She is passionate about being a part of the creation of new works in Melbourne and nationally.

LUCY ANSELL
PHOENIX

Lucy is a multidisciplinary artist of Afro-Caribbean/English descent, currently based on unceded Wurundjeri land. She trained at the Victorian College of the Arts, graduating in 2018. Recently, she featured in Robert Connolly's *The Dry 2: Force of Nature* and Binge Original Series: *Strife*. Past live productions include *Hour of the Wolf* (dir. Matthew Sutton, Malthouse Theatre), *Escaped Alone/What If If Only* (dir. Anne-Louise Sarks, Melbourne Theatre Company), *Your Name Means Dream* (dir. Kat Henry, Red Stitch) and *Harry Potter and the Cursed Child*, Melbourne (Michael Cassel Group). Other stage credits include *Wild Cherries* (dir. Beng Oh), Patalog Theatre's *Far Away* (dir. Cass Fumi) and *She Is Vigilante* (written by Chanella Macri and co-dir. by Krystalla Pearce and Bridget Balodis) which she later received a Green Room award for. In her own works, Lu aims to interrogate imagined constructs and explore the nexus between art and therapy.

CAROLINE LEE
RAE

Caroline has been working professionally as a performer for over thirty years. Most recently she has appeared in *Honour*, *Your Name Means Dream*, *Ssshh*, *Wittenoom*, *The Cane*, *Single Ladies*, *Escaped Alone*, *Dance Nation*, *Colder*, *Suddenly Last Summer*, *Sunshine*, *Jurassica* and *Wet House* (Red Stitch); played Lola Montez in *The Exotic Lives* of *Lola Montez* with Finucane and Smith, which also toured Victoria and New South Wales; performed in *All I'm Saying* written by Ben Brooker at La Mama; toured Victoria and New South Wales with *Jurassica*; performed in *Conviction*, written by Zoey Moonbeam Dawson and directed by Declan Greene; toured regional Victoria in *Waking Up Dead* and toured China with Finucane and Smith in The Flood. She has also performed in Bell Shakespeare's production of *Phèdre*; *The Trouble with Harry*, *The Carnival of Mysteries*, and *The Minotaur Trilogy* for the Melbourne International Arts Festival; *Waking Up Dead*, directed by Susie Dee and written by Trudy Hellier at fortyfivedownstairs; played the role of Sylvia Plath in Barry Dickins' *A Kind of Fabulous Hatred*; and appeared in *Small Metal Objects* in New York, Toronto, Vancouver and Cardiff with Back to Back Theatre. Recent film and television appearances include playing Jean in *The Newsreader 1, 2 and 3*; and roles in *Miss Fisher's Modern Murder Mysteries*, and *The Dressmaker*. Caroline has won four Green Room awards and is a well known, and awarded, narrator of talking books.

LAILA THAKER
NEL

Laila Thaker is a staunch Torres Strait Islander (Meriam Wagadagam) and Indian (Ratlamwali) Actor. Since graduating with a BA in Theatre (JCU Cairns) and Cert IV in Film and Television (TAW Brisbane), she has been cast in various roles from Shakespeare to Sarah Kane. Her works include, *The Return* (Malthouse Theatre), *Coconut Woman* (YIRRAMBOI), *Viral* (ILBIJERRI), *RFDS* (Channel 7), *Apple Cider Vinegar* (Netflix), *Five Bedrooms* (Paramount), *Wentworth* (Foxtel), *Informer 3838* (Nine Network), *My Life is Murder* (Channel Ten), *Bad Mothers* (Nine Network), *The Queen and I* (NITV/ABC), *House Husbands* (Nine Network) and LA feature films *San Andreas* and *Christmas Downunder*. Her role in *Prayers to Broken Stone* (Boutique Theatre) won her Best Emerging Indigenous Artist for the Melbourne Fringe Awards (2017). As a member of ICMEAA, Laila continues to empower First Nations voices and affirm Blak storytelling that's meaningful in the arts.

RED STITCH ACTORS' THEATRE

Red Stitch is a creative hub, offering scope for artists to make work they are passionate about in a sector where such opportunities are limited. As the ensemble and executives of Red Stitch, we provide a platform where leading practitioners can hone their craft and take risks, and emerging artists can work alongside mid-career and seasoned professionals. We play a vital role in the development and presentation of new Australian works through our INK playwriting program, promoting local voices alongside acclaimed contemporary international work which may not otherwise be seen by local audiences.

www.redstitch.net

Red Stitch would like to thank the following supporters who generously contribute to our INK program.

www.currency.com.au

Visit Currency Press' website now to:
- Order books
- Browse through our full list of titles including plays, screenplays, theory and reference/criticism, performance handbooks, educational texts and more
- Choose a play for your school or performance group by cast specs
- Seek performance rights
- Find out about performing arts news and sign up for our newsletter
- For students: read our study guides
- For teachers: access free curriculum information and teacher notes

We are also on Facebook and Instagram (@currencypress). Join the conversation!

The performing arts publisher

www.ingramcontent.com/pod-product-compliance
Lightning Source LLC
Chambersburg PA
LVHW062122080426
734CB00012B/2956